Maui
on the
Rocks II

A Modern Bar Guide

Janette Paiva

Hanalani Maui
P.O. Box 2914
Wailuku, HI, USA 96793

International Standard Book Number: 0-9673532-0-3
Library of Congress Card Number: 99-95283

Paiva, Janette
Maui on the Rocks II

Maui on the Rocks II contains more than 250 drink recipes in eight major categories. Recipes and categories are designed to meet the needs of the professional mixologist as well as others interested in preparing mixed drinks—from island residents to tourists.

Front & Back Cover Photo Objects: Hemera Technologies Inc.

Second Printing, 1989
Third Printing, 1993
Fourth Printing, Revised and Enlarged, 1999

Printed in United States of America

Published by

Hanalani Maui
P.O. Box 2914
Wailuku, HI, USA 96793

ACKNOWLEDGMENTS

Thank you to the many people and companies that have made this book possible: Allen Nishiyama, Krislyn Elvenia, Susan Kawamoto, Cheryl Bajinting, Ethel Leval, Applegate and Associates, Koho's Grill and Bar, my new friend dawn (Photography by dawn) and Victor C. Pellegrino of Maui arThoughts Company.

I especially want to extend my gratitude to my husband "K", my mom and dad, Jason and Eva Ambrose, my brother Jason, and my children Ui and Hanalei for all their support.

CONTENTS

INTRODUCTION

Maui on the Rocks—A Modern Bar Guide came into being in 1985. It has been reprinted twice, and this 1999 fourth printing has been revised and enlarged. New drinks have been added, and changes have been made to reflect modern tastes and drink preferences. Thus, I have added **II** to the title—**Maui on the Rocks II—A Modern Bar Guide**.

There are many reasons why this book came into being, and why a newly revised and enlarged fourth printing come to be. First, Hawai'i is a unique visitor destination, and people come here from around the world. They look forward to the colorful, delightful, and tasty drinks prepared in our local bars and restaurants. In fact, just sipping a tropical drink under a palm tree in Hawai'i is not an unfamiliar dream for visitors. And it can come true by using the recipes in **Maui on the Rocks II—A Modern Bar Guide**.

Maui on the Rocks II—A Modern Bar Guide is not only a delightful collection of intriguing and unique drinks. It is also a useful tool for the novice and professional. Simple, clear, and step-by-step recipes will result in perfection for everyone—from the most inexperienced to the advanced mixologist.

These beverage recipes are my favorites. Neither Hanalani Maui nor I make any claim that all the recipes are original. When possible, credit has been given where credit is due. In most cases, recipes have been modified, including ingredients, amounts, and directions.

Finally, I want to add a word of caution. Enjoy these wonderful concoctions slowly. Know your limit. And don't drink and drive. If you wish, many of the drinks in **Maui on the Rocks II—A Modern Bar Guide** can be made without adding liquor, or the quantity of liquor can be reduced. Whatever you decide, drink wisely, safely, and still have fun (whether at a bar or restaurant, your condo or hotel, or at home).

With fondest aloha,
Janette Pavia
Wailuku, Maui, Hawai'i
1999

Tropicals

LAVA FLOW

> 1 oz. Rum
> 1 oz. Coconut Syrup
> 2 oz. Pineapple Juice
> 1/2 oz. Sweet & Sour
> 1/2 oz. Milk
> 1/4 Cup Frozen Strawberries (Pure'ed)

Blend everything except strawberries with 1 1/2 cups small ice cubes. Pour strawberries on bottom of 12 oz. stemmed cocktail glass followed with blended mixture. The strawberries should make the LAVA FLOW effect. I have found that using strawberries that are frozen in heavy syrup are the best. Just thaw them out. Garnish with a fresh strawberry.

CHI CHI

> 1 oz. Vodka
> 1 oz. Coconut Syrup
> 1/2 oz. Sweet & Sour
> 2 oz. Pineapple Juice
> 1/2 oz. Milk

Blend with 1 1/2 cups small ice cubes until smooth. Serve in a 12 oz. cocktail glass with a pineapple wedge and a cherry for garnish.

MAI TAI

1 oz. Light Rum
1 oz. Sweet & Sour
1 1/2 oz. Pineapple Juice
1/4 oz. Orgeat Syrup
1/2 oz. Orange Curacao
1 oz. Dark Rum (Top Float)

Serve over ice in a 12 oz. cocktail glass. Garnish with a wedge of pineapple and a cherry.

PINA COLADA

1 oz. Light Rum
1 oz. Coconut Syrup
2 oz. Pineapple Juice
1/2 oz. Sweet & Sour
1/2 oz. Milk

Blend with 1 1/2 cups small ice cubes and serve in a 12 oz. cocktail glass. Garnish with a wedge of pineapple and a cherry.

BLUE HAWAII

1 oz. Light Rum
1/2 oz. Blue Curacao
1 oz. Sweet & Sour
2 oz. Pineapple Juice
1/2 oz. Milk

Blend with 1 1/2 cups small ice cubes and serve in a 12 oz. cocktail glass. Garnish with a wedge of pineapple and a cherry.

MAKENA BEACH

1/2 oz. Vodka
1/2 oz. Gin
1/2 oz. Light Rum
1/2 oz. Blue Curacao
1 oz. Sweet & Sour
1 oz. Pineapple Juice

Served over ice in a 12 oz. cocktail glass. Garnish with a wedge of pineapple and a cherry.

I BELIEVE DENISE IS RESPONSIBLE FOR THIS CONCOCTION. SHE HAS AGREED TO BE ON CALL AFTER YOU HAVE TRIED A FEW OF THESE. MAHALO, DENISE.

OAHU SUNSET

1 oz. Compari
1 oz. Light Rum
1 oz. Dark Rum
2 oz. Passion Juice
2 oz. Pineapple Juice

Serve over ice in a 12 oz. cocktail glass.

THIS DRINK RECIPE IS FROM ANTHONY LAUDANO FROM WOODBRIDGE, CONNECTICUT. MAHALO, ANTHONY.

POI POUNDER

1 oz. Vodka
3 oz. Guava Juice

Serve on the rocks.

SUN DOWNER

1 oz. Cognac
3/4 oz. Galliano
3/4 oz. Cointreau
1 oz. Sweet & Sour

Serve over ice in a 7 oz. cocktail glass.

YOU WILL SEE THE SUN GO DOWN-BUT WILL YOU EVER SEE IT COME UP AGAIN?

BORA BORA

1 oz. Light Rum
3/4 oz. Grand Marnier
1/2 oz. Banana Liqueur
Pineapple Juice
Coke

Serve over ice in a chimney glass. Liquor goes in first, then fill with pineapple juice and top off with a splash of coke.

KONA BLEND

3/4 oz. Galliano
3/4 oz. Coffee Liqueur
1 oz. Milk

This can be served blended with 1 cup small ice cubes or over ice in a rocks glass.

BOTH DELICIOUS..........

HAWAIIAN PUNCH

1/2 oz. Vodka
1/2 oz. Amaretto
1/2 oz. Southern Comfort
1/2 oz. Sloe Gin
1/2 oz. Grenadine
Pineapple Juice Fill

Start with grenadine then pour remaining ingredients over ice in a chimney glass. Garnish with pineapple wedge and a cherry.

THIS IS ONE PUNCH THAT WILL SURELY BE FELT IN THE MORNING.

KONA MAC

3/4 oz. Kona Coffee Liqueur
3/4 oz. Macadamia Nut Liqueur
1 oz. Milk

Blend with 1 cup small ice cubes and serve in a 7 oz. cocktail glass.

MAALAEA MUD FLAT

1 oz. Vodka
1/2 oz. Dark Creme De Cacao
1/2 oz. Irish Cream
Fill with club soda

Serve on the rocks in a 7 oz. cocktail glass.

YOU'LL SLIP AND S—L—I—D—E AFTER A FEW OF THESE. MAHALO, RANDY.

BETWEEN THE SHEETS

3/4 oz. Light Rum
3/4 oz. Brandy
1/2 oz. Triple Sec
1 oz. Sweet & Sour

Blend with 1 cup small ice cubes and serve in a 7 oz. Cocktail glass.

PLANTER'S PUNCH

1 1/2 oz. 151 Rum
1/2 oz. Grenadine
3/4 oz. Orange Juice
3/4 oz. Pineapple Juice
3/4 oz. Sweet & Sour
1/2 oz. Dark Rum (Float)

Serve this over the rocks in a bucket glass, saving the dark rum for a top float. Garnish with a pineapple wedge and cherry.

GET YOUR FEET FIRMLY PLANTED BEFORE YOU DRINK ONE OF THESE.

SUFFERING BASTARD

1 oz. Brandy
1 oz. Vodka
3 Dashes Bitters
1 oz. Sweet & Sour
Splash of 7UP

Serve over ice in a 7 oz. cocktail glass.

HAWAIIAN SUNSET

1 1/2 oz. Light Rum
3 oz. Passion-Orange-Guava Juice
Juice of 1/2 Lime

Serve blended with 1 1/2 small ice cubes or on the rocks in a chimney glass. Garnish with a pineapple wedge and a cherry.

SINGAPORE SLING

1 oz. Gin
1 1/2 oz. Sweet & Sour
1/2 oz. Grenadine
1/2 oz. Cherry Brandy
Club soda

Pour grenadine, sweet & sour and gin over crushed ice and stir. Fill with club soda and top off with cherry brandy. Serve in a chimney glass and garnish with a lime wheel speared with a cherry.

A SLING IS WHAT YOU'LL NEED FOR YOUR HEAD AFTER A COUPLE OF THESE.

MISSIONARY'S DOWNFALL

1 1/4 oz. Light Rum
1/2 oz. Apricot Liqueur
1/4 oz. Rock Candy Syrup
1 oz. Sweet & Sour
2 oz. Pineapple Juice

Blend all ingredients with 1 1/2 cups of small ice cubes and serve in a large cocktail glass. Garnish with a pineapple wedge and cherry.

LANAI LADY

1 1/4 oz. Light Rum
1/2 oz. White Creme De Cacao
1/2 oz. Banana Liqueur
1/2 oz. Galliano
2 oz. Orange Juice
2 oz. Cream
1 Ripe Banana

Blend everything with 1 1/2 cups small ice cubes and serve in a 12 oz. cocktail glass. Garnish with Pineapple wedge and a cherry.

BEAUTIFUL WAILEA

1 oz. Rum
1/2 oz. Cherry Brandy
1/2 oz. Amaretto
1 oz. Orange Juice
1 oz. Pineapple Juice
1 oz. Sweet & Sour

Serve over ice in a 12 oz. cocktail glass. Garnish with a pineapple wedge and cherry.

HAWAIIAN COOLER

1 oz. Light Rum
1 oz. Sweet & Sour
4 oz. Pineapple Juice
1/2 oz. Green Creme de Menthe (Float)

Serve over ice in a chimney glass. Pour Creme de Menthe on the top as a float.

NAVY GROG

1 oz. Light Rum
1/2 oz. Brandy
1 oz. Dark Rum (Float)
2 oz. Grapefruit Juice
2 oz. Sweet & Sour
1/2 oz. Orgeat Syrup
1/2 oz. Grenadine

Serve over ice in a bucket glass, floating the dark rum on top.

ZOMBIE

1 oz. Dark Rum
1 oz. 151 Rum (Float)
Dash Bitters
1 oz. Pineapple Juice
1 oz. Sweet & Sour
1/4 oz. Grenadine

Serve in a chimney glass with crushed ice. Save the 151 rum for a top float. Garnish with a pineapple wedge and cherry.

YOU'LL SURELY LOOK SPOOKY AFTER ONE OF THESE.

SCORPION

1 oz. Brandy
1 oz. Light Rum
1 oz. Sweet & Sour
1 oz. Pineapple Juice
1/2 oz. Rock Candy Syrup

Blend with 1 1/2 cups small ice cubes and serve in a 12 oz. cocktail glass. Garnish with a pineapple wedge and cherry.

GETTING STUNG IS ONLY HALF THE FUN.

KAHLUA SHAKE

1 oz. Rum
3/4 oz. Kahlua
1/2 oz. Coconut Syrup
1 oz. Milk

Blend with 1 cup small ice cubes until smooth, and serve in a chimney glass.

FOGCUTTER

1/2 oz. Light Rum
1/2 oz. Brandy
1/2 oz. Gin
1/4 oz. Dry Vermouth
1 oz. Sweet & Sour
2 oz. Orange Juice
1/2 oz. Rock Candy Syrup
1/2 oz. Orgeat Syrup

Serve over crushed ice in a tall cocktail glass, saving the vermouth for a top float. Garnish with a lime wheel speared with a cherry.

THINGS MAY LOOK A LITTLE FOGGY AFTER A FEW OF THESE.

PINK CORAL

1 1/4 oz. Light Rum
2 oz. Pineapple Juice
1 oz. Sweet & Sour
1/4 oz. Grenadine
Dash Milk

Serve over crushed ice in a 12 oz. cocktail glass.

TROPICAL ITCH

1 1/4 oz. 151 Rum
1/2 oz. Bourbon
1/2 oz. Cherry Brandy
1 oz. Sweet & Sour
1 oz. Orange Juice
1 oz. Pineapple Juice

Serve over crushed ice in a chimney glass, saving the cherry brandy for a top float. Garnish with a pineapple wedge and a cherry.

A BACK SCRATCHER WILL ALSO BE NEEDED AFTER YOUR TROPICAL ITCH TAKES EFFECT.

PASSIONATE INU

1 oz. Light Rum
1/2 oz. Vodka
1/2 oz. Apricot Brandy
2 oz. Orange Juice
1 oz. Sweet & Sour
1/4 oz. Grenadine

Serve over ice in a 12 oz. cocktail glass.

LOLA GRANOLA

1 1/2 oz. Amaretto
1/2 oz. Coffee Liqueur
1 oz. Half & Half
3 oz. Orange Juice
1/2 of a Ripe Banana

Blend with 1 1/2 cups small ice cubes. Serve in a 12 oz. cocktail glass.

YELLOW BIRD

1 1/4 oz. Light Rum
3/4 oz. Galliano
1/2 oz. Cointreau
2 oz. Orange Juice
1 oz. Sweet & Sour

Serve over ice in a 12 oz. cocktail glass.

MAUI ICE TEA

1/2 oz. Light Rum
1/2 oz. Vodka
1/2 oz. Gin
2 oz. Sweet & Sour
2 oz. Orange Juice
1/2 oz. Dark Rum (Float)

Serve over ice in a 12 oz. cocktail glass.

MOVE OVER LONG ISLAND. MAUI'S GOT ITS OWN LO-
CAL ICE TEA. MAHALO, DENISE.

STRAWBERRY COLADA

1 oz. Light Rum
1 oz. Coconut Syrup
1/4 Cup Frozen Strawberries with Syrup
1 oz. Sweet & Sour
1/2 oz. Milk

Blend with 1 1/2 cups small ice cubes and serve in a 12 oz.
cocktail glass. Garnish with a wedge of pineapple and a fresh strawberry.

AMARETTO COLADA

1 oz. Amaretto
1 oz. Coconut Syrup
2 oz. Pineapple Juice
1/2 oz. Sweet & Sour
1/2 oz. Milk

Blend with 1 1/2 cups small ice cubes and serve in a 12 oz. cocktail glass. Garnish with a wedge of pineapple and a cherry.

MAUI LADY

1 oz. Peach Brandy
1/2 oz. Light Rum
1/2 oz. Galliano
2 oz. Pineapple Juice

Serve over ice in a 7 oz. cocktail glass.

HURRICANE

3/4 oz. Light Rum
3/4 oz. Dark Rum
1 oz. Orange Juice
1 oz. Pineapple Juice
Dash Grenadine

Serve over ice in a 7 oz. cocktail glass.

THIS ONE WILL SURELY BLOW YOU AWAY.

BANANA JAVA

1 oz. Coffee Liqueur
1/2 oz. Creme de Banana
1 Ripe Banana
1 oz. Milk

Blend with 1 cup small ice cubes until smooth and serve in a 7 oz. cocktail glass.

WAIKAPU PUNCH

1 oz. 151 Rum
1 oz. Pineapple Juice
1 oz. Orange Juice
1 oz. Guava Juice
1 oz. Passion Fruit Juice
1 oz. Dark Rum (Float)

Served in a 12 oz. cocktail glass over ice.

THIS DELICIOUS CONCOCTION, FROM RENEE', IS SO GOOD THAT IT WON A LOCAL DRINK RECIPE CONTEST. MAHALO, RENEE'

RUM PUNCH

1 1/2 oz. White Rum
2 oz. Orange Juice
1 oz. Sweet and Sour
1/2 oz. Orange Curacao
1/4 oz. Grenadine

Serve over ice or blended with 1 1/2 cups small ice cubes. Use a bucket glass. Garnish with a pineapple wedge and a cherry.

DA WALL CLIMBER

1 oz. 100 Proof Vodka
1/2 oz. White Rum
3 oz. Strawberry Guava Nectar (made from concentrate)
Lime Juice (2 fresh limes)

Serve over ice or blended with 1 1/2 cups small ice cubes. Use a bucket glass. Garnish with a fresh strawberry.

THIS DRINK RECIPE WAS CREATED ESPECIALLY FOR MY CO-WORKERS, WHO LITERALLY "CLIMB THE WALLS" AT WORK. CHEERS TO ART, DANNY, JO ANN, LAURA, LEI, SAM, ALEXIS, FOY, SUSAN, ELSA, ANNA AND "DA BOSS", JERRY. THE NAMES SHOULD HAVE BEEN CHANGED TO PROTECT THE "NOT SO" INNOCENT! LET'S NOT FORGET FRANK AND VINCE WHO FINALLY MADE IT "OVER DA WALL."

Daiquiris & Margaritas

STRAWBERRY DAIQUIRI

> 1 oz. Light Rum
> 1/4 cup Frozen Strawberries
> 1/2 oz. Strawberry Liqueur (Optional)
> 2 oz. Sweet & Sour

Blend with 1 1/2 cups small ice cubes. Serve in a 12 oz. cocktail glass. Garnish with a pineapple wedge and a cherry or fresh strawberry.

PEACH DAIQUIRI

> 1 oz. Light Rum
> 1/4 cup Fresh or Canned Peaches
> 1/2 oz. Peach Liqueur
> 2 oz. Sweet & Sour

Blend with 1 1/2 cups small ice cubes. Serve in a 12 oz. cocktail glass. Garnish with a pineapple wedge and a cherry.

GUAVA DAIQUIRI

> 1 oz. Light Rum
> 3 oz. Guava Juice
> 1 oz. Sweet & Sour

Blend with 1 1/2 cups small ice cubes and serve in a 12 oz. cocktail glass. Garnish with a pineapple wedge and a cherry.

BANANA DAIQUIRI

    1 oz. Light Rum
    1/2 oz. Creme de Banana
    1 oz. Sweet & Sour
    1/2 oz. Milk
    1 Ripe Banana

Blend with 1 1/2 cups small ice cubes. Serve in a 12 oz. cocktail glass. Garnish with a pineapple wedge and a cherry.

PINEAPPLE DAIQUIRI

    1 oz. Light Rum
    1/4 cup Fresh or Canned Pineapple Chunks
    2 oz. Pineapple Juice
    1 oz. Sweet & Sour

Blend with 1 1/2 cups small ice cubes. Serve in a 12 oz. cocktail glass. Garnish with a wedge of pineapple and a cherry.

PINEAPPLE & STRAWBERRY DAIQUIRI

    1 oz. Light Rum
    1/2 oz. Strawberry Liqueur (Optional)
    1/4 cup Fresh or Canned Pineapple Chunks
    1/4 cup Frozen Strawberries
    2 oz. Pineapple Juice

Blend everything with 1 1/2 cups small ice cubes and serve in a 12 oz. cocktail glass. Garnish with a wedge of pineapple and a fresh strawberry.

BERRY BANANA DAIQUIRI

1 oz. Light Rum
1/2 oz. Banana Liqueur
1 oz. Sweet & Sour
1/4 cup Frozen Strawberries
1/2 Milk
Half a Ripe Banana

Blend with 1 1/2 cups small ice cubes and serve in a 12 oz. cocktail glass. Garnish with a fresh strawberry.

LIME DAIQUIRI

1 oz. Light Rum
3 oz. Sweet & Sour
1/2 oz. Lime Juice

Blend with 1 1/2 cups small ice cubes and serve in a 12 oz. cocktail glass. Garnish with a lime wheel.

MELON DAIQUIRI

1 oz. Light Rum
3/4 oz. Melon Liqueur
2 oz. Sweet & Sour

Blend with 1 1/2 cups small ice cubes and serve in a 12 oz. cocktail glass. Garnish with a lime wheel.

MANGO DAIQUIRI

1 oz. Light Rum
1/4 cup Ripe Mango Chunks
2 oz. Sweet and Sour

Blend with 1 1/2 cups small ice cubes and serve in a 12 oz. cocktail glass. Garnish with a firm wedge of mango. Hint: if you freeze some mango wedges ahead of time, they will help to make your daiquiri frostier.

MINT DAIQUIRI

1 oz. Light Rum
2 oz. Sweet and Sour
1/2 oz. White Creme De Menthe

Blend with 1 1/2 cups small ice cubes and serve in a 12 oz. cocktail glass. Use 1 oz. of creme de menthe to create a stronger mint flavor. Garnish with mint leaves, a lime wheel, or both.

MARGARITA

1 oz. Tequila
1/2 oz. Triple Sec
2 oz. Sweet & Sour
1/4 oz. Lime Juice

For a very frosty and refreshing drink, add 1 1/2 cups small ice cubes to these ingredients and blend. Serve in a 12 oz. glass with a salt rim. Garnish with a fresh lime wheel.

WASTING AWAY IN MARGARITAVILLE IS EVEN BETTER WHEN ON MAUI.

STRAWBERRY MARGARITA

1 oz. Tequila
1/2 oz. Triple Sec
1/4 cup Frozen Strawberries
2 oz. Sweet & Sour

Blend together with 1 1/2 cups small ice cubes and serve in a 12 oz. cocktail glass. Sugar may be used on rim of glass if desired. Garnish with a fresh lime wheel.

PINEAPPLE MARGARITA

1 oz. Tequila
1/2 oz. Triple Sec
1 oz. Sweet and Sour
1 oz. Pineapple Juice
1/4 Cup Fresh or Canned Pineapple Chunks

Blend with 1 1/2 cups small ice cubes and serve in a 12 oz. cocktail glass with a sugared rim if desired. Garnish with a wedge of pineapple.

PEACH MARGARITA

1 oz. Tequila
1/2 oz. Peach Liqueur
2 oz. Sweet & Sour
1/4 cup Fresh or Canned Peaches

Blend together with 1 1/2 cups small ice cubes. Serve in a 12 oz. cocktail glass. Sugar may be used on the rim of the glass if desired. Garnish with a fresh lime wheel.

BANANA MARGARITA

1 oz. Tequila
1/2 oz. Creme de Banana
2 oz. Sweet & Sour
1 Ripe Banana

Blend with 1 1/2 cups small ice cubes and serve in a 12 oz. cocktail glass. Sugar may be used on rim. Garnish with a fresh lime wheel.

MELON MARGARITA

1 oz. Tequila
3/4 oz. Melon Liqueur
2 oz. Sweet & Sour

Blend with 1 1/2 cups small ice cubes and serve in a 12 oz. cocktail glass. Sugar may be used on the rim if desired. Garnish with a fresh lime wheel.

TOP SHELF MARGARITA

1 oz. Gold Tequila
1/4 oz. Cointreau
1/2 oz. Grand Marnier (Float)
2 oz. Sweet & Sour
Splash Lime Juice

Blend all ingredients except Grand Marnier with 1 1/2 cups small ice cubes. Pour into a 12 oz. salt rimmed glass and top off with Grand Marnier. Garnish with a lime wheel.

ITALIAN MARGARITA

> 1 oz. Brandy
> 1/2 oz. Amaretto
> 2 oz. Sweet & Sour
> Splash Lime Juice

Blend all ingredients in blender with 1 1/2 cups small ice cubes and serve in a 12 oz. salt rimmed glass. Garnish with a lime wheel.

SAY 'ARRIVEDERCI' AFTER A FEW OF THESE.

BLUE MARGARITA

> 1 oz. Tequila
> 3/4 oz. Blue Curacao
> 2 oz. Sweet & Sour
> Splash of Lime Juice

Blend with 1 1/2 cups small ice cubes and serve in a 12 oz. salt rimmed glass. Garnish with a lime wheel.

Cocktails

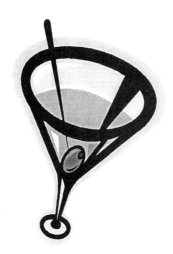

BLOODY MARY

1 oz. Vodka
Tobasco (2 or 3 drops)
Worcestershire (1/4 tsp.)
Sprinkle Celery Salt
Sprinkle Pepper
Tomato Juice Fill

Serve over ice in a bucket glass with a salted rim. Garnish with celery stalk and a fresh lime squeeze.

TERRIFIC FOR THE MORNING AFTER.

BLOODY BULL

1 oz. Vodka
2 or 3 drops Tobasco
1/4 tsp. Worcestershire
Sprinkle Pepper
Sprinkle Celery Salt
1/2 Fill Bull shot
1/2 Fill Tomato Juice

Serve over ice in a bucket glass with a salted rim. Garnish with celery stalk and a fresh lime squeeze.

OLE!

SCREWDRIVER

1 oz. Vodka
Orange Juice Fill

Serve over ice in a 7 oz. cocktail glass.

BLOODY MARIA

1 oz. Tequila
Sprinkle Celery Salt
Sprinkle Pepper
2 or 3 Drops Tobasco
1/4 tsp. Worcestershire
Fill with Tomato Juice

Serve over ice in a bucket glass, with a salted rim. Garnish with a celery stalk and a squeeze of lime.

SALTY DOG

1 oz. Vodka
Grapefruit Juice Fill

Serve with a salted rim over ice in a 7 oz. cocktail glass.

YOUR BARK WILL BE A LOT WORSE THAN YOUR BITE WITH A FEW OF THESE.

ASS KICKER

1 6 oz. can Minute Maid Frozen Lemon Concentrate
6 oz. Blended Whiskey
6 oz. Water
1 tbs. Maraschino Cherry Juice

Mix in a blender with ice or serve over ice in a rocks glass. Garnish with a cherry and lemon slice.

THIS DRINK IS FROM VIC PELLEGRINO'S FRIEND, LARRY DALY, WHO WARNED THAT THE FIRST ONE GOES DOWN EASY, BUT THE SECOND ONE KICKS BUTT!

GREYHOUND

1 oz. Vodka
Grapefruit Juice Fill

Serve over ice in a 7 oz. cocktail glass. (Also known as a Bull-dog)

SLOE SCREW

1 oz. Sloe Gin
Orange Juice Fill

Serve over ice in a 7 oz. cocktail glass. (Also known as a Co-bra)

ITALIAN SCREW

1 oz. Galliano
Orange Juice Fill

Serve over ice in a 7 oz. cocktail glass.

MAMA MIA!

SLOE COMFORTABLE SCREW

3/4 oz. Sloe Gin
3/4 oz. Southern Comfort
Orange Juice Fill

Serve over ice in a 7 oz. cocktail glass.

HARVEY WALL BANGER

1 oz. Vodka
1/2 oz. Galliano (Float)
Orange Juice Fill

Served over ice in a chimney glass.

POOR HARVEY. YOU WOULD THINK BY NOW HE WOULD
HAVE LEARNED HIS LESSON. . .

COBRA

1 oz. Vodka
Orange Juice Fill

Serve over ice in a 7 oz. cocktail glass. (Also known as a Sloe
Screw)

FUZZY NAVEL

1 oz. Vodka
3/4 oz. Peach Schnapps
Orange Juice Fill

Serve over ice in a 7 oz. cocktail glass.

BON JOVI

1 oz. Vodka
1/2 oz. Peach Schnapps
Fill with 1/2 orange juice and 1/2 cranberry juice.

Serve over ice in a 7 oz. cocktail glass.

BEACH BUM

1 oz. Vodka
1/2 oz. Melon Liqueur
Fill with cranberry juice

Serve over ice in a 7 oz. cocktail glass.

COOLAID

1/2 oz. Amaretto
1/2 oz. Southern Comfort
1/2 oz. Melon Liqueur
2 oz. Cranberry Juice

Serve over ice in a 7 oz. cocktail glass or pour over ice to chill, then strain into a chilled cocktail glass.

WHICHEVER WAY IS COOL FOR YOU.

KILLER COOLAID

1/2 oz. Vodka
1/2 oz. Southern Comfort
1/2 oz. Melon Liqueur
1/2 oz. Amaretto
Fill Cranberry Juice

Serve over ice in a 7 oz. cocktail glass or pour over ice to chill, then strain into a chilled cocktail glass.

YOU BE THE JUDGE: IS IT A KILLER OR NOT??????

CAPE COD

1 oz. Vodka
Fill Cranberry Juice

Serve over ice in a 7 oz. cocktail glass.

MADRAS

1 oz. Vodka
1 1/2 oz. Orange Juice
1 1/2 oz. Cranberry Juice

Serve over ice in a 7 oz. cocktail glass.

SEA BREEZE

1 oz. Vodka
2 oz. Cranberry Juice
Splash Grapefruit Juice

Serve over ice in a 7 oz. cocktail glass.

ORANGE BLOSSOM

1 oz. Gin
2 oz. Orange Juice
1/4 oz. Rock Candy Syrup

Serve over crushed ice in a 7 oz. cocktail glass.

LEMON DROP

1 oz. Vodka
Lemon Juice (Squeeze 2 wedges of fresh lemon)
1 tsp. Sugar

Pour vodka, lemon juice and 1/2 tsp. sugar over ice and stir. Coat the rim of a chilled martini glass with the remaining 1/2 tsp. sugar. Do this by rubbing a wedge of lemon around rim of martini glass then turn it upside down on the sugar. Strain vodka mixture into martini glass. Garnish with a lemon wheel.

BULLDOG

1 oz. Vodka
Grapefruit Juice Fill

Served over ice in a 7 oz. cocktail glass. (Also known as a Greyhound)

APPLE BLOSSOM

1 oz. Apple Schnapps
Fill Cranberry Juice

Serve over ice in a 7 oz. cocktail glass.

A FROOT LOOP

1/2 oz. Grand Marnier
1/2 oz. Melon Liqueur
1/2 oz. Peach Schnapps
2 oz. Cranberry Juice

Serve over ice in 7 oz. cocktail glass.

THIS DRINK IS BROUGHT TO YOU BY M. SMITH AND HIS FRIENDS FROM RENO. MAHALO, GUYS.

FREDDY FUDPUCKER

1 1/4 oz. Tequila
2 1/2 oz. Orange Juice
Float 1/2 oz. Galliano

Serve over ice in a 7 oz. cocktail glass.

BY THE POOL

3/4 oz. Peach Schnapps
3/4 oz. Melon Liqueur
1/2 Orange Juice Fill
1/2 7UP Fill
Serve over ice in a chimney glass.

MAY ALSO BE SERVED BY A WATERFALL.

57 T-BIRD

1/2 oz. Southern Comfort
1/2 oz. Peach Schnapps
Splash Orange Juice

Pour over ice, shake and strain into a chilled glass or serve over ice.

FUZZY MONGOOSE

1 oz. Vodka
1/2 oz. Peach Schnapps
1/2 oz. Melon Liqueur
2 oz. Pineapple Juice
Dash Club Soda

Serve over ice in a 7 oz. cocktail glass.

CATAMARAN

1 oz. Vodka
1 oz. Light Rum
1 oz. Sweet & Sour
2 oz. Pineapple Juice

Serve in a bucket glass over ice or blend with 1 1/2 cups small ice cubes.

JUNGLE GYM

1 1/4 oz. Vodka
1/2 oz. Banana Liqueur
1 oz. Milk

Serve over ice in a rocks glass.

GET SWINGING WITH A FEW THESE.

KISS IN THE DARK

1 oz. Gin
1 oz. Cherry Brandy
1 oz. Dry Vermouth

Stir with ice and strain into a chilled cocktail glass.

ALABAMA SLAMMER

1/2 oz. Sloe Gin
1/2 oz. Southern Comfort
1/2 oz. Amaretto
2 oz. Orange Juice

Serve over ice in a rocks glass.

WEASEL

1 oz. Southern Comfort
3/4 oz. Amaretto
7UP Fill

Serve over ice in a 7 oz. cocktail glass. Rub a fresh lime wedge along rim of glass.

SLAM DUNK

1 1/4 oz. Southern Comfort
1 oz. Cranberry Juice
1 oz. Orange Juice

Serve over ice in a rocks glass.

ORANGE SLICE

1 oz. Amaretto
1 oz. Orange Juice
1 oz. Milk

Pour over ice and serve in a rocks glass with a slice of orange.

ORGASM

1/2 oz. Amaretto
1/2 oz. Irish Cream
1/2 oz. Coffee Liqueur
1 oz. Milk

Blend with 1 cup small ice cubes and serve in a 7 oz. cocktail glass.

NO COMMENT.

ORANG-U-TANG

1 oz. Tequila
3/4 oz. Amaretto
Orange Juice Fill

Served over ice in a 7 oz. cocktail glass.

RED SILK PANTIES

1 oz. Vodka
3/4 oz. Peach Schnapps
2 oz. Cranberry Juice

Serve over ice in a rocks glass.

SEX ON THE BEACH

1 1/2 oz. Peach Schnapps
Fill Cranberry Juice

Serve over ice in a 7 oz. cocktail glass.

WATCH OUT WHEN THE TIDE ROLLS IN.

RAZZTINI

1 oz. Razzberry Liqueur
1/2 oz. Vodka
3/4 oz. Sweet & Sour
3/4 oz. 7UP

Pour over ice in a mixing glass and stir until chilled. Strain into a chilled martini glass. May also be served over ice.

SEX MACHINE

1 oz. Vodka
1/2 oz. Coffee Liqueur
1/2 oz. Grand Marnier
1/2 oz. Milk (Float)

Serve over ice in a rocks glass.

YOU MIGHT NEED SERVICING AFTER A FEW OF THESE.

DIRTY MOTHER

1 1/2 oz. Brandy
3/4 oz. Kahlua

Serve over ice in a rocks glass.
(Add milk and get a DIRTY WHITE MOTHER)

BRAVE BULL

1 oz. Tequila
3/4 oz. Kahlua

Served over ice in a rocks glass

BLACK RUSSIAN

1 oz. Vodka
3/4 oz. Kahlua

Served over ice in a rocks glass.

WHITE RUSSIAN

1 oz. Vodka
3/4 oz. Kahlua
2 oz. Milk

Served over ice in a 7 oz. cocktail glass.

MIND ERASER

1 oz. Vodka
1 oz. Kahlua
7Up Fill

Served layered over ice in a 7 oz. cocktail glass.

SEX ON THE ROCKS

1 oz. Kahlua
1 oz. Grand Marnier
2 oz. Milk

Serve over ice in a 7 oz. cocktail glass.

AFTER A FEW OF THESE YOU WON'T EVEN FEEL THE ROCKS.

KAHLUA & MILK

1 oz. Kahlua
3 oz. Milk

Serve over ice in a 7 oz. cocktail glass.

SEPARATOR

1 oz. Brandy
3/4 oz. Kahlua
Milk Fill

Serve over ice in a 7 oz. cocktail glass.

KEEP AN EYE ON YOUR LEGS...THEY MIGHT GO IN THE OPPOSITE DIRECTION.

BROWN COW

1 oz. Dark Creme de Cacao
3 oz. Milk

Served over ice in a 7 oz. cocktail glass.

GODMOTHER

1 oz. Vodka
3/4 oz. Amaretto

Serve over ice in a rocks glass.

GODFATHER

1 oz. Scotch
3/4 oz. Amaretto

Serve over ice in a rocks glass.

SCARLET O'HARA

1 1/4 oz. Southern Comfort
Cranberry Juice Fill

Serve over ice in a 7 oz. cocktail glass.

SCREAMING ORGASM

1/2 oz. Amaretto
1/2 oz. Kahlua
1/2 oz. Tequila
1/2 oz. Irish Cream
1 oz. Milk

Blend with 1 cup small ice cubes and serve in 7 oz. cocktail glass.

CAN'T TOUCH THIS.

TOOTSIE ROLL

3/4 oz. Coffee Liqueur
3/4 oz. Dark Creme de Cacao
Orange Juice Fill

Serve over ice in a 7 oz. cocktail glass.

OBLIZER

3/4 oz. Kahlua
3/4 oz. Amaretto
2 oz. Milk

Serve over ice in a 7 oz. cocktail glass.

WATERMELON

1 1/2 oz. Melon Liqueur
Fill with Cranberry Juice

Serve over ice in a 7 oz. cocktail glass.

THIS CANNOT BE COUNTED AS YOUR DAILY REQUIRE-MENT OF FRUIT.

RED SNAPPER

1 oz. Vodka
1/2 oz. Kahlua
1/2 oz. Amaretto
2 oz. Milk

Serve over ice in a 7 oz. cocktail glass.

ALICE IN WONDERLAND

1/2 oz. Tia Maria
1/2 oz. Gold Tequila
1/2 oz. Grand Marnier

Serve over ice in a rocks glass.

YOU'LL KNOW YOU'VE HAD ENOUGH WHEN YOU ASK "I WONDER WHERE I AM".

APRICOT SCREWDRIVER

1 1/2 oz. Apricot Brandy
Orange Juice Fill

Serve over ice in a 7 oz. cocktail glass.

LONDON PICK-ME-UP

1 oz. Brandy
3 Drops Bitters
Club Soda Fill

Pour over ice and serve in a 7 oz. cocktail glass.

RUSTY NAIL

1 oz. Scotch
1/2 oz. Drambuie

Served up in a snifter or pour over ice in a rocks glass.

IF YOU'RE NOT CAREFUL YOU WILL SURELY GET LOCK JAW.

CUBA LIBRA

1 oz. White Rum
Coke Fill

Serve over ice in a 7 oz. cocktail glass with a squeeze of fresh lime.

SLAMMER

1 1/2 oz. Tequila
1/2 oz. Ginger Ale

Serve in a 2 oz. shot glass with no ice. It should be served immediately so the ale doesn't get flat. The way to drink this is to slam it down on a hard surface and drink it as it fizzes.

TRY TO BE QUIET WHEN SLAMMING OR YOU'LL HAVE TO MAKE ONE FOR EVERYONE IN THE HOUSE.

KAMIKAZE

1 oz. 100 Proof Vodka
1/2 oz. Triple Sec
1/2 oz. Lime Juice

Pour over ice and stir. Strain into a well chilled cocktail glass. Garnish with a lime wheel.

SOFT WHITE SPIDER

1 oz. Vodka
1/2 oz. White Creme De Menthe
Club Soda or Milk Fill

Serve over ice in a 7 oz. cocktail glass with a squeeze of lime.

FINE TUNER

1 1/4 oz. Vodka
1/2 oz. Peach Schnapps

Pour over ice, stir and strain into a chilled cocktail glass.

JUST ONLY ONE MORE

1 oz. Vodka
1 oz. Dubonnet
1 oz. Club Soda

Serve over ice in a rocks glass.

DAN ALWAYS SAID, "JUST ONLY ONE MORE, PLEASE."
MAHALO, DAN.

SNOW MAN

1 oz. Vodka
1/2 oz. Peppermint Schnapps

Pour over ice, stir and strain into a chilled cocktail glass.

JAKE

1 oz. Jack Daniels
Coke Fill

Serve over ice in a 7 oz. cocktail glass.

GREEN APPLE

3/4 oz. Melon Liqueur
3/4 oz. Apple Schnapps

Serve over ice in a rocks glass.

WOO WOO

1 1/4 oz. Vodka
3/4 oz. Peach Schnapps
Cranberry Juice Fill

Serve over ice in a 7 oz. cocktail glass.

MAHALO, SCOTTY.

SWAMP WATER

1 oz. Vodka
1/2 oz. Melon Liqueur
Pineapple Juice Fill

Serve over ice in a 7 oz. cocktail glass.

GREEN WEENIE

1 oz. Peppermint Schnapps
3/4 oz. Melon Liqueur

Stir with ice and strain into a chilled cocktail glass.

THIS IS ONE DRINK THAT MAY BE EMBARRASSING TO ORDER WHEN YOU ASK, "MAY I HAVE A GREEN WEENIE PLEASE?" YOU'RE SURE TO GET A SNICKER.

MELON BALL

1 oz. Vodka
3/4 oz. Melon Liqueur
Orange Juice Fill

Pour over ice in a 7 oz. cocktail glass.

PEARL HARBOR

1 oz. Vodka
3/4 oz. Melon Liqueur
Sweet & Sour Fill

Pour over ice in a chimney glass. Serve with a pineapple wedge and cherry.

MELONCHOLY BABY

1 1/2 oz. Melon Liqueur

Served over ice in a rocks glass with 2 or 3 squeezed fresh lime wedges.

SILK PANTIES

1 oz. Vodka
1/2 oz. Peach Schnapps

Stir with ice and strain into a chilled cocktail glass.

SMOOTH...!

BAY BREEZE

1 1/4 oz. Vodka
Fill with 1/2 cranberry juice and 1/2 pineapple juice

Serve over ice in a 7 oz. cocktail glass.

GOLDEN RAZZBERRY

1 oz. Gold Tequila
3/4 oz. Razzberry Schnapps
1 oz. Sweet & Sour
Dash Grenadine
Club Soda Fill

Serve over ice in a chimney glass.

SNAPPER

1 1/2 oz. Gin
1 1/2 oz. White Creme de Menthe

Stir with ice and strain into a chilled cocktail glass.

WATCH OUT. YOU MIGHT JUST GET HOOKED.

GREEN LIZARD

1 oz. 151 Rum
1/2 oz. Green Chartreuse

Served up in a snifter.

WATCH OUT. TOO MANY OF THESE AND YOU'LL ALSO BE
SLIDING ON YOUR BELLY.

RUM RUNNER

1 oz. Dark Rum
1/2 oz. Light Rum
1/2 oz. Blackberry
1/2 oz. Banana Liqueur
1 oz. Sweet & Sour
1 oz. Orange Juice
Dash Grenadine

Served over ice in a bucket glass.

SNAKE BITE

1 1/4 oz. Yukon Jack
1/2 oz. Lime Juice

Pour over ice and stir. Strain into a chilled cocktail glass.

WHEN THIS ONE BITES, IT'S ALL OVER

ELECTRIC GATORADE

1/2 oz. Vodka
1/2 oz. Gin
1/2 oz. Rum
1/2 oz. Tequila
Fill 1/2 Sweet & Sour & 1/2 Club Soda
1/2 oz. Melon Liqueur (Float)

Served over ice in a bucket glass.

LONG ISLAND ICE TEA

1/2 oz. Vodka
1/2 oz. Gin
1/2 oz. Rum
1/2 oz. Tequila
1/2 oz. Triple Sec
1 oz. Sweet & Sour
Coke Fill

Pour over ice in chimney glass and serve with a squeeze of fresh lime.

LONG BEACH ICE TEA

1/2 oz. Vodka
1/2 oz. Gin
1/2 oz. Rum
1/2 oz. Tequila
1/2 oz. Triple Sec
1 oz. Sweet & Sour
Cranberry Juice Fill

Pour over ice in a chimney glass and serve with a squeeze of fresh lime.

TEQUILA SUNRISE

1 1/4 oz. Tequila
1/4 oz. Grenadine
Orange Juice Fill

Fill 7 oz. cocktail glass with ice. Pour grenadine first, then tequila and fill with orange juice.

WHAT A WAY TO START YOUR DAY.

COLLINS

JOHN: 1 oz. Bourbon
2 oz. Sweet & Sour
Splash 7UP & Club Soda Fill

VODKA: 1 oz. Vodka
2 oz. Sweet & Sour
Splash 7UP & Club Soda Fill

TOM: 1 oz. Gin
2 oz. Sweet & Sour
Splash 7UP & Club Soda Fill

BERRY: 1 oz. Vodka
1 oz. Sweet & Sour
2 oz. Cranberry Juice & Club Soda Fill

All Collins are served over ice in a chimney glass with a fresh lime squeeze and a cherry.

VODKA TWISTER

1 1/2 oz. Vodka
1/2 oz. Lime Juice
7UP Fill

Serve over ice in a chimney glass.

SLIPPERY NIPPLE

1 oz. Hazelnut Liqueur
1 oz. Irish Cream

Served over ice in a rocks glass.

SMITH & KERNS

1 oz. Coffee Liqueur
3 oz. Milk
Splash Club Soda

Served over ice in a 7 oz. cocktail glass.

LASER BEAM

1/2 oz. Amaretto
1/2 oz. Licorice Liqueur
1/2 oz. Jack Daniels
1/2 oz. Peppermint Schnapps

Served over crushed ice.

GIMLET

1 oz. Gin , Vodka or Tequila
1 oz. Lime Juice

Any one of these liquors will make a great gimlet. Served in a rocks glass over ice or chilled and served up in a gimlet glass. Garnish with a lime wheel.

REMEMBER, I SAID ANY 1, NOT ALL.

MARTINI

1 1/2 oz. Gin
1/4 oz. Dry Vermouth

Pour over ice and stir. Strain into a chilled martini glass or serve over ice in a rocks glass. Garnish with a couple of green olives. (Note: To make a dry martini, use less dry vermouth. A very dry martini would be served with only a couple of drops of vermouth.)

GIBSON

1 1/2 oz. Gin
1/4 oz. Dry Vermouth

Pour over ice and stir. Strain into a chilled martini glass or serve over ice in a rocks glass. Garnish with a couple of cocktail onions.

MANHATTAN

1 1/2 oz. Bourbon
1/4 oz. Sweet Vermouth

Pour over ice and stir. Strain into a chilled Manhattan glass or serve over ice in a rocks glass. Garnish with a cherry.

DRY MANHATTAN

1 1/2 oz. Bourbon
1/4 oz. Dry Vermouth

Pour over ice and stir. Strain into a chilled Manhattan glass or serve over ice in a rocks glass. Garnish with a couple of green olives.

PERFECT MANHATTAN

1 1/4 oz. Bourbon
1/4 oz. Sweet Vermouth
1/4 oz. Dry Vermouth

Pour over ice and stir. Strain into a chilled Manhattan glass or serve over ice in a rocks glass. Garnish with a twist of lemon.

PRESBYTERIAN

1 oz. Bourbon
Ginger Ale
Club Soda

Fill with equal parts of ginger ale and club soda. Serve over ice in a rocks glass. Garnish with a twist of lemon.

OLD FASHION

1 oz. Bourbon
1/2 tsp. Rock Candy Syrup
2 Dashes Bitters
Club Soda

Pour syrup and bitters in Old-Fashioned or rocks glass and stir. Add soda and mix. Add ice and bourbon. Garnish with lemon twist and cherry.

ROB ROY

1 1/4 oz. Scotch
1/4 oz. Sweet Vermouth

Pour over ice and stir. Strain into a chilled cocktail glass or serve over ice in a rocks glass. Garnish with a twist of lemon peel and cherry.
Variations:
(DRY)
1 1/4 oz. Scotch
1/4 oz. Dry Vermouth
Garnish: Green Olives

(PERFECT)
1 1/4 oz. Scotch
1/4 oz. Dry Vermouth
1/4 oz. Sweet Vermouth
Garnish: Lemon Twist

Both the Dry and Perfect Rob Roy are prepared the same way as the Rob Roy above.

AMARETTO SOUR

1 oz. Amaretto
2 oz. Sweet & Sour

Blend with 1 cup small ice cubes and serve in a 7 oz. cocktail glass. Garnish with a cherry.

MELON SOUR

1 oz. Melon Liqueur
2 oz. Sweet & Sour

Blend with 1 cup small ice cubes and serve in a 7 oz. cocktail glass. Garnish with a cherry.

WHISKEY SOUR

1 oz. Bourbon
2 oz. Sweet & Sour

Blend with 1 cup small ice cubes and serve in a 7 oz. cocktail glass. Garnish with a cherry.

VODKA SOUR

1 oz. Vodka
2 oz. Sweet & Sour

Blend with 1 cup small ice cubes and serve in a 7 oz. cocktail glass. Garnish with a cherry.

ITALIAN BOOT

1 oz. Vodka
1/2 oz. Amaretto
2 oz. Orange Juice
Splash Club Soda
1/2 oz. Galliano (Float)

Served over ice in a 7 oz. cocktail glass. Galliano should be poured slowly on top, as a float. Garnish with a cherry.

THIS IS ONE BOOT THAT WILL KICK YOUR _____ IF YOU DON'T WATCH OUT!

BACARDI COCKTAIL

1 oz. Bacardi Light Rum
2 oz. Sweet & Sour
1/4 oz. Grenadine

Blend with 1 cup small ice cubes and serve in a 7 oz. cocktail glass.

PINK LADY

1 oz. Gin
2 oz. Milk
1/4 oz. Grenadine

Blend with 1 cup small ice cubes and serve in a 7 oz. cocktail glass.

RAMOZ FIZZ

1 oz. Gin
1 oz. Orange Juice
1/2 oz. Sweet & Sour
1/4 oz. Milk
Orange Flower Water
Dash of Rock Candy Syrup
1 Egg White

Blend everything except the orange flower water with 1 cup small ice cubes. Put a few drops of orange flower water in a bucket glass and roll it around, then pour in blended mixture.

SLOE GIN FIZZ

1 oz. Sloe Gin
2 oz. Sweet & Sour
Dash of Club Soda

Blend gin and sweet & sour with 1 cup small ice cubes, pour into chimney glass and top with club soda. Garnish with a cherry.

GRASSHOPPER

3/4 oz. Green Creme De Menthe
3/4 oz. White Creme De Menthe
1 oz. Milk

Blend with 1 cup small ice cubes and serve in a 7 oz. cocktail glass.

WALKING WILL BE HARD ENOUGH WITH A FEW OF THESE. DON'T EVEN ATTEMPT TO HOP.

ALEXANDER 2

1 oz. Sloe Gin
3/4 oz. Light Creme De Cacao
1/2 oz. Milk

Blend with 1 cup small ice cubes and serve in a 7 oz. cocktail glass.

VELVET HAMMER

3/4 oz. Coffee Liqueur
3/4 oz. Cointreau
2 oz. Milk

Blend with 1 cup small ice cubes and serve in a 7 oz. cocktail glass.

ROOT BEER FLOAT

1 oz. Vodka
1/2 oz. Coffee Liqueur
1/2 oz. Galliano
1/2 oz. Milk
Coke

Blend everything except soda with 1 cup small ice cubes. Pour into a chimney glass and top of with soda.

BE CAREFUL, THIS ONE IS SO "ONO".

QUAALUDE

1/2 oz. Vodka
1/2 oz. South Comfort
1/2 oz. Melon Liqueur
2 oz. Orange Juice
Dash Grenadine

Blend with 1 cup small ice cubes and serve in a 7 oz. cocktail glass.

THIS ONE IS DEFINITELY NOT PRESCRIBED BY THE DOCTOR.

RUSSIAN QUAALUDE

1/2 oz. Coffee Liqueur
1/2 oz. Amaretto
1/2 oz. Hazelnut Liqueur
1/2 oz. Irish Cream
1 oz. Milk

Blend with 1 cup small ice cubes and serve in a 7 oz. cocktail glass.

UNIVERSE

1 oz. Vodka
1/2 oz. Pistachio
1/2 oz. Melon Liqueur
1 1/2 oz. Pineapple Juice
1/2 oz. Roses Lime Juice

Blend with 1 1/2 cups small ice cubes and serve in a bucket glass.

CREAM SICLE

3/4 oz. Orange Curacao
3/4 oz. Triple Sec
3/4 oz. Orange Juice
1/2 oz. Milk

Blend with 1 cup small ice cubes and serve in a 7 oz. cocktail glass.

ENJOY IT SLOWLY. THIS ONE WON'T MELT.

BRANDY ALEXANDER

1 oz. Brandy
3/4 oz. Dark Creme De Cacao
1 oz. Milk or 1 Scoop Vanilla Ice Cream

Combine with 1 cup small ice cubes and blend well. Serve in a 12 oz. stem glass with a sprinkle of nutmeg on top.

GOLDEN CADILLAC

3/4 oz. Galliano
3/4 oz. White Creme De Cacao
2 oz. Milk

Blend with 1 cup small ice cubes and serve in a 7 oz. cocktail glass.

FACE IT. THIS IS AS CLOSE AS YOU'LL GET TO A REAL GOLDEN CADILLAC.

RENO SLIMER

1 1/4 oz. Melon Liqueur
Milk Fill

Serve over ice in a 7 oz. cocktail glass.

NOTHING SLIMY ABOUT THIS DRINK. AT LEAST THAT'S
WHAT MATTHEW FROM RENO SAID. MAHALO, MATTHEW.

SIDE CAR

1 oz. Brandy
3/4 oz. Triple Sec
1 oz. Roses Lime Juice

Blend with 1 cup small ice cubes and serve in a 7 oz. cocktail
glass with a sugar rim.

TOASTED ALMOND

3/4 oz. Amaretto
3/4 oz. Coffee Liqueur
3 oz. Milk

Serve over ice in a 7 oz. cocktail glass.

Wine Cocktails

SPRITZER

4 oz. White Wine
2 oz. Club Soda

Served over ice in a bucket glass. Garnish with a squeeze of fresh lime.

RED WINE COOLER

4 oz. Burgundy
1/2 oz. Sweet & Sour
7UP Fill

Served over ice in a bucket glass. Garnish with a squeeze of fresh lime.

WHITE WINE COOLER

4 oz. White Wine
1/2 oz. Sweet & Sour
7UP Fill

Served over ice in a bucket glass. Garnish with a squeeze of fresh lime.

KIR

6 oz. White Wine
1/2 oz. Creme De Cassis

Serve chilled in a wine glass.

NAPA SUNSET

4 oz. White Wine
2 oz. Orange Juice

Serve over ice in a bucket glass. Garnish with a fresh slice of orange.

SANGRIA

3 oz. Burgundy
1 oz. Cherry Brandy
1 1/2 oz. Orange Juice
1 oz. Sweet & Sour

Served over ice in a 12 oz. stemmed cocktail glass. Float fresh orange and lemon wheels for garnish.

MIMOSA

4 oz. Champagne
2 oz. Orange Juice

Serve in a chilled champagne glass.

CHAMPAGNE COCKTAIL

2 Dashes Bitters
Pinch of Sugar
Fill with champagne

Serve in a chilled champagne glass with a twist of lemon.

ROSE' WINE COOLER

4 oz. Rose' Wine
1/2 oz. Sweet and Sour
7UP Fill

Serve over ice in a bucket glass. Garnish with a squeeze of fresh lime.

TROPICAL COOLER

4 oz. Rose' Wine
1 oz. Guava Nectar
1/2 Sweet and Sour
7UP Fill

Serve over ice in a bucket glass. Garnish with a lime wheel.

Cordials
&
After Dinner Drinks

AFTER FIVE

1/2 oz. Coffee Liqueur
1/2 oz. Irish Cream
1/2 oz. Peppermint Schnapps
1/2 oz. Vodka

Pouring over the back of a bar spoon, layer these ingredients in the order they are listed. Use any small stemmed glass.

THERE IS A REASON FOR THE NAME OF THIS DRINK & IT'S NOT 5 A.M.

B- 51

1/2 oz. Coffee Liqueur
1/2 oz. Irish Cream

Layer coffee liqueur, then Irish Cream, using the back of a bar spoon. Serve in a 1 oz. cordial or pony glass.

B-52

1/3 oz. Coffee Liqueur
1/3 oz. Irish Cream
1/3 oz. Grand Marnier

Pour each liqueur in the order that they're listed off the back of a bar spoon. Serve in a 1 oz. cordial or pony glass.

A B C

1/3 oz. Amaretto
1/3 oz. Baileys Irish Cream
1/3 oz. Cointreau

Pour each liqueur in the order that they're listed off the back of a bar spoon. Serve in a 1 oz. cordial or pony glass.

THIS ONE IS DEFINITELY NOT FOR PRE- SCHOOLERS.

MUD SLIDE

1/3 oz. Coffee Liqueur
1/3 oz. Irish Cream
1/3 oz. Vodka

Pour each liqueur slowly in the order that they're listed off the back of a bar spoon. Serve in a 1 oz. cordial or pony glass.

KING ALFONSE

3/4 oz. Dark Creme De Cacao
1/4 oz. Cream

Float cream on top by gently pouring it over the back of a bar spoon. Serve in a 1 oz. cordial or pony glass.

E.T.

1/3 oz. Irish Cream
1/3 oz. Melon Liqueur
1/3 oz. Vodka

Pour each liqueur slowly in the order that they're listed off the back of a bar spoon. Serve in a 1 oz. cordial or pony glass.

BANANA SPLIT

1/3 oz. Dark Creme De Cacao
1/3 oz. Strawberry Liqueur
1/3 oz. Creme De Banana

Pour each liqueur in the order that they're listed off the back of a bar spoon. Serve in a 1 oz. cordial or pony glass. You may put a little whipped cream on top, if you want to.

PARACHUTER

1/3 oz. Coffee Liqueur
1/3 oz. Irish Cream
1/3 oz. Creme De Banana

Pour each liqueur slowly in the order that they're listed off the back of a bar spoon. Serve in a 1 oz. cordial or pony glass.

TOO MANY OF THESE AND YOU WILL GLIDE SLOWLY TO THE GROUND.

747

1/3 oz. Coffee Liqueur
1/3 oz. Irish Cream
1/3 oz. Hazel Nut Liqueur

Pour each liqueur slowly in the order that they're listed off the back of a bar spoon. Serve in a 1 oz. cordial or pony glass.

WHEN YOU START TO FEEL TURBULENCE, I THINK YOU HAVE HAD ENOUGH.

CONCORD

1/3 oz. Coffee Liqueur
1/3 oz. Irish Cream
1/3 oz. 151 Rum

Pour each liqueur slowly in the order that they're listed off the back of a bar spoon. Serve in a 1 oz. cordial or pony glass.

AMARIST

3/4 oz. Amaretto
3/4 oz. Grand Marnier

Serve in a snifter glass. No ice.

STINGER

1 oz. Brandy
3/4 oz. White Creme De Menthe

Serve over ice in a rocks glass or in a snifter, no ice.

JELLY BEAN

1 oz. Blackberry Brandy
1 oz. Anisette Liqueur

Serve in a snifter. No ice.

IF YOU LIKE BLACK JELLY BEANS YOU'LL LOVE THIS, IT TASTES EXACTLY LIKE THEM.... MAHALO, MARY PAT

SNOW SHOE

1/2 oz. Brandy
1/2 oz. Peppermint Schnapps

Serve in a shot glass with the brandy on top.

THIS ONE WILL SURELY CUT THE CHILL ON A COLD WINTER'S NIGHT..........

PEPPERMINT PATTY

3/4 oz. Peppermint Schnapps
3/4 oz. Coffee Liqueur

Serve over ice in a rocks glass.

BEAUTIFUL

3/4 oz. Grand Marnier
3/4 oz. Cognac

Serve in a snifter. No ice.

THE NAME DESCRIBES IT ALL.

APPLE PIE

3/4 oz. Cinnamon Schnapps
3/4 oz. Apple Schnapps

Serve in a snifter. No ice.

JUST LIKE MOM USE TO MAKE.

AFTER DINNER COCKTAIL

1 oz. Apricot Brandy
1 oz. Orange Curacao
Juice from one lemon wedge.

Pour over ice and stir. Strain into a 4 oz. cocktail glass.

SICILIAN KISS

3/4 oz. Southern Comfort
3/4 oz. Amaretto

Serve in a snifter. No ice.

THIS IN ONE KISS THAT WILL SURELY WEAKEN YOUR KNEES.

MELLOW YELLOW

3/4 oz. Southern Comfort
3/4 oz. Galliano

Serve over ice in a rocks glass or up in a snifter.

LAMPEDINA

1 oz. Brandy
1/2 oz. Triple Sec
1/4 oz. Coffee Liqueur

Pour all ingredients in a snifter and flambe. Then add 1 oz. cream. (optional)

GREAT FOR AFTER DINNER, BEFORE OR DURING OR. . . MAHALO, SCOTTY.

B & B

3/4 oz. Brandy
3/4 oz. Benedictine

Serve in a snifter. No ice.

BRANDY SPECIAL

1 1/4 oz. Apricot Brandy
1/2 oz. Triple Sec

Serve in a snifter or if preferred, pour over ice, stir, and strain into a 4 oz. cocktail glass.

Coffee
&
Hot Drinks

JAMAICAN COFFEE

1 oz. Tia Maria
3/4 oz. Dark Rum
1 cup Hot Coffee

Top with whipped cream and a cherry.

IRISH COFFEE

1 oz. Irish Whiskey
1/4 oz. Rock Candy Syrup or 1/2 tsp. Sugar
1 cup Hot Coffee

Top with whipped cream, green creme de menthe and a cherry.

WHEN YOU SEE THE LEPRECHAUN, START DRINKING BLACK COFFEE—<u>STRONG</u> BLACK COFFEE!

SPANISH COFFEE

3/4 oz. Tia Maria
3/4 oz. Coffee Liqueur
1 cup Hot Coffee

Top with whipped cream and a cherry.

SI, SEÑOR.

MEXICAN COFFEE

3/4 oz. Tequila
3/4 oz. Coffee Liqueur
1 cup Hot Coffee

Top with whipped cream and a cherry.

COFFEE KISS

1/2 oz. Irish Cream
1/2 oz. Dark Creme De Cacao
1/2 oz. Triple Sec
1 cup Hot Coffee

Top with whipped cream and a cherry.

HOW SWEET IT IS.

ITALIAN COFFEE

1 oz. Brandy
1/2 oz. Tuaca
1/2 oz. Amaretto
1 cup Hot Coffee

Top with whipped cream and a cherry.

MINT MOCHA

3/4 oz. White Creme De Menthe
3/4 oz. Dark Creme De Cacao
1 cup Hot Coffee

Top with whipped cream, chocolate shavings, and a cherry.

CAFE AMARETTO

1 oz. Amaretto
1 cup Hot Coffee

Top with whipped cream and a cherry.

SLEEPY PENGUIN

2 oz. Hot Coffee
1 oz. Creme De Cacao
Pour into mug
Blend: 1 small banana
1 oz. Creme De Banana
2 oz. Milk

Pour blended mixture into coffee and creme de cacao. Top with whipped cream and a sprinkle of nutmeg.

MONTE CRISTO

3/4 oz. Grand Marnier
3/4 oz. Coffee Liqueur
1 cup Hot Coffee

Top with whipped cream and a cherry.

SPICED ORANGE COFFEE

1 oz. Triple Sec
1 cup Hot Coffee

Top with whipped cream and a sprinkle of cinnamon.

KONA MAC ROYALE

1 oz. Kona Coffee Liqueur
1 oz. Macadamia Nut Liqueur
1 cup Hot Coffee

Top with whipped cream, chopped macadamia nuts and a cherry.

KIOKI COFFEE

1 oz. Brandy
3/4 oz. Coffee Liqueur
1 cup Hot Coffee

Top with whipped cream and a cherry.

KAHLUA COFFEE

1 1/4 oz. Kahlua
1 cup Hot Coffee

Top with whipped cream and a cherry.

CALYPSO COFFEE

1 oz. Coffee Liqueur
1/2 oz. Tia Maria
1 cup Hot Coffee

Top with whipped cream and a cherry.

HAIRY PALM

3/4 oz. Peppermint Schnapps
3/4 oz. Coffee Liqueur
1 cup Hot Coffee

Top with whipped cream and a cherry. A little green creme de menthe may be poured over whipped cream for an added touch.

CREAM NUT

3/4 oz. Hazelnut Liqueur
3/4 oz. Irish Cream
1 cup Hot Coffee

Top with whipped cream and a cherry.

KAPALUA COFFEE

1/2 oz. Grand Marnier
1/2 oz. Tia Maria
1/2 oz. Dark Rum
1 cup Hot Coffee

Top with whipped cream and a cherry.

CAFE ROYALE

1 1/4 oz. Brandy
1/2 Tsp. Sugar
1 cup Hot Coffee

Top with whipped cream and a cherry.

TIA GRANDE

3/4 oz. Tia Maria
3/4 oz. Grand Marnier

Pour into 1 cup hot tea.

HOT TODDY

1 oz. Bourbon
1/4 oz. Rock Candy Syrup or 1/2 tsp. Sugar
1/2 oz. Sweet & Sour

Pour into mug filled with 2/3 cups hot water and float a lemon wheel.

BLACKBERRY COFFEE

1 oz. Blackberry Flavored Brandy
1 cup Hot Coffee

Top with whipped cream and a cherry.

COCONUT ALMOND COFFEE

1 oz. Amaretto
1/2 oz. Dark Creme De Cocoa
1/2 oz. Coconut Syrup
1 cup Hot Coffee

Top with whipped cream, coconut flakes and a cherry.

ITALIAN STALLION

1 oz. Anisette
1 cup Hot Coffee

Top with whipped cream and a cherry.

CHRISTMAS JOY

3 oz. of Espresso (chilled)
1 cup of Eggnog
2 oz. of Nocello Liqueur

Pour over ice. Top with a light sprinkling of powdered chocolate, cinnamon, and nutmeg.

KONA SURPRISE

1 Cup of Kona Coffee (chilled)
1 tbs. Coconut Syrup
1/4 cup Milk
1 oz. of Kahlua

Pour over crushed ice. Garnish with a sprinkling of grated coconut.

ESPRESSO DELIGHT

4 1/2 oz. of French Roast Espresso (hot)
1 oz. of Dark Rum
1 Scoop of Vanilla Ice Cream

Top hot espresso with ice cream and a sprinkling of powdered chocolate.

THIS IS A GOOD MORNING-NIGHT AFTER OR AN AFTER LUNCH WAKER-UPPER.

Ice Cream Drinks

DREAMSICLE

1 1/4 oz. Amaretto
1 Large Scoop Vanilla Ice Cream (Softened)
2 oz. Orange Juice

Blend with 1/2 cup small ice cubes until smooth. Top with whipped cream and an orange wheel on top.

DREAM ON. . .

GOLDEN DREAM

3/4 oz. Galliano
3/4 oz. Cointreau
1 oz. Orange Juice
1 Large Scoop Vanilla Ice Cream (Softened)

Blend with 1/2 cup small ice cubes until smooth. Top with whipped cream and a cherry.

THIS IS ONE DREAM THAT YOU WON'T WANT TO END.

STRAWBERRY SHORTCAKE

1 1/4 oz. Amaretto
1/4 cup Frozen Strawberries (Sweetened)
1 Large Scoop Vanilla Ice Cream (Softened)
1 oz. Milk

Blend with 1/2 cup small ice cubes. Top with whipped cream and a fresh strawberry.

ICE CREAM SANDWICH

1 oz. White Creme De Cacao
1 Large Scoop Vanilla Ice Cream (Softened)
1 oz. Milk
2 Chocolate Wafer Cookies With Cream Filling

Blend until smooth with 1/2 cup small ice cubes. Top with whipped cream, a whole cookie and a cherry.

MILK AND COOKIES WILL NEVER BE THE SAME.

SWAN SHAKE

3/4 oz. Irish Cream
3/4 oz. Peach Liqueur
1/4 cup Sliced Peaches (Frozen O.K.)
1 Large Scoop Vanilla Ice Cream (Softened)
1 oz. Milk

Blend with 1/2 cup small ice cubes until smooth. Top with whipped cream and a cherry.

YOU'LL FEEL GRACEFUL AS A SWAN AFTER A COUPLE OF THESE. LET'S HOPE YOU'LL ACT LIKE ONE.

BIT-O-HONEY

3/4 oz. Irish Cream
3/4 oz. White Creme De Cacao
1 oz. Milk
1 Large Scoop Vanilla Ice Cream (Softened)

Blend with 1/2 cups small ice cubes until smooth. Top with whipped cream and a cherry.

ALMOND JOY

3/4 oz. Amaretto
3/4 oz. Coffee Liqueur
1 oz. Milk
1 Large Scoop Vanilla Ice Cream (Softened)

Blend with 1/2 cups small ice cubes until smooth. Top off with whipped cream and a cherry.

SPECIAL MAHALO TO KOHO'S GRILL & BAR FOR THESE DELICIOUS ICE CREAM RECIPES. VISIT THEM AT KAAHUMANU CENTER & IN NAPILI ON MAUI.

Homemade Liqueurs

ALMOND LIQUEUR

1/4 cup Water
1 cup Light Corn Syrup
1 cup Sugar
2 cups Vodka
5 tsp. Almond Extract

Combine water, corn syrup & sugar in saucepan and bring to boil. Stir until sugar is dissolved. Remove from heat and cool approximately 20 minutes. Add vodka and almond extract. Makes 1 quart.

IRISH CREAM

1/2 Pint Whipping Cream
1 Can Condensed Milk
2 tbs. Chocolate Syrup
1/2 tsp. Almond Extract
1 tsp. Vanilla
4 Eggs
1 3/4 cups Brandy

Blend all ingredients well in blender. Makes 1 quart. Refrigeration Required.

PEPPERMINT SCHNAPPS

1/4 cup Water
1 cup Light Corn Syrup
1 cup Sugar
2 cups Vodka
2 tsp. Peppermint Extract

Bring water to boil in saucepan, add corn syrup and sugar. Stir until dissolved. Remove from heat and cool. Add vodka and peppermint extract. Makes 1 quart.

YOU MAY SUBSTITUTE AND FLAVOR EXTRACTS SUCH AS PEACH, ROOT BEER, ETC...

COFFEE LIQUEUR

1/4 cup Water
3 tbs. Dark Instant Coffee
1 cup Light Corn Syrup
1 cup Sugar
2 cups Vodka
4 tsp. Vanilla

Bring water to boil in saucepan, add coffee and stir until dissolved. Add corn syrup and sugar. Stir until blended well. Remove from heat and cool for about 20 minutes, then add vodka and vanilla. Makes 1 quart.

MAHALO, MOM MEIERDIERCKS.

APRICOT LIQUEUR

1 lb. Dried Apricots
1 lb. Rock Candy
Vodka

Place alternate layers of dried apricots and rock candy in a large jar. Pour in vodka until covered. Any inexpensive vodka will due. Cover and store for 2-3 months. Strain the apricot liqueur into a bottle. Use the remaining apricots to top ice cream desserts (keep refrigerated).

THANKS TO VIC AND WALLETTE PELLEGRINO FOR THIS SPECIALTY.

HELPFUL HINTS

Most ingredients for the recipes in **Maui on the Rocks II—A Modern Bar Guide** can be found easily at your favorite supermarket or liquor store. You can use brand name products in your recipes or substitute the wide variety of other brands available today.

The homemade recipes for coffee, amaretto, schnapps, and Irish creme will surely enhance the flavor of all recipes calling for them. These substitutes may also be used. Sweet and Sour: one half teaspoon of sugar and one half ounce of lemon juice will make approximately three fourths of an once of sweet and sour. Rock Candy Syrup: one teaspoon of sugar and two teaspoons of water will make one half once of syrup.

When you are planning a cocktail party or simply setting up a home bar, there are several important items you will need. Once you have decided on the kinds of cocktails you plan to make for your guests, look up the recipes for them in **Maui on the Rocks II—A Modern Bar Guide.** Make a list of the liquors, liqueurs and mixers (e.g., milk, juices, etc...) you will need. In addition, make sure you have on hand:

- ice cubes
- ice scoop
- ice bucket
- cocktail glasses
- cocktail napkins
- plastic stirring rods
- short and long straws
- garnishes: limes, lemons, cherries, pineapples, etc.
- spices
- mixing glass and cocktail strainer
- long bar spoon for floating and stirring
- measuring cup
- 1 ounce jigger
- spouts for pouring liquors

INDEX

ABOUT THE AUTHOR

Janette (Ambrose) Paiva was born and raised in Wailuku, Maui. After graduating from St. Anthony High School in 1974, she continued her studies at Maui Community College.

She has worked as a bartender for fourteen years and perfected many drinks that have been enjoyed by local and visitor clientele.

In 1985, she published her first book, **Maui on the Rocks, A Modern Bar Guide**. The title, a registered trade name, was suggested by a friend, Allen Nishiyama, and Janette knew it would attract a wide audience—to those who enjoy a well-made drink and to bartenders who want to please their Maui, Hawaiian Island, and Mainland customers.

Maui on the Rocks, A Modern Bar Guide, has been reprinted two times, and has sold more than 12,000 copies. This new 1999 edition is a 4th printing, appropriately titled **Maui on the Rocks II, A Modern Bar Guide.** It is revised, edited and enlarged, with more than 250 drinks. Many have been shared with her customers and with friends who have helped her make changes that reflect careful adjustments in contents or amounts.

Janette maintains her expertise in drink making by helping to host parties and luaus.

She is married to Harold Kaleiolani Paiva, and they have two children, Hanalei and Uilani.

HOW TO OBTAIN COPIES OF MAUI ON THE ROCKS II— A MODERN BAR GUIDE

■ Request copies of **Maui on the Rocks II—A Modern Bar Guide**, (ISBN 0-9673532-0-3) from your local bookstore. If unavailable, please use the order form below, and we will ship your order. United States Postal Service prices and book prices are subject to change without notice.

------------------ Copy, Clip, and Mail ------------------

ORDER FORM

❑ Please send me _____ copy (ies) of
Maui on the Rocks II—A Modern Bar Guide

❑ Please include payment with this order:
$9.95 per book plus $3.00 S&H. Add
$.50 S&H for each additional copy.
Make checks payable to HANALANI MAUI

❑ Amount Enclosed: $ _____

❑ Mail your order to: Hanalani Maui
P.O. Box 2914
Wailuku, HI, USA 96793

❑ Ship my order to: (Print or type clearly)

Your Name: _____
Address: _____
City: _____
State: _____
Country: _____
Zip: _____